Get a DISCOUNT!

By Mary Hertz Scarbrough

CELEBRATION PRESS

Pearson Learning Group

Contents

Be a Smart Shopper

Did you ever want to buy something, but you didn't have enough money at the time? That can be frustrating. It's hard to wait while you try to save money. What can you do?

You can be a smart shopper. You can watch for deals. Do you ever watch television, listen to the radio, use the Internet, or glance at a newspaper? Have you ever noticed a store window sign showing a sale or seen coupons for the grocery store? If you've done some of these things, you already have some smart shopper skills!

Local stores often have sales.

sale
sale price will be charged at checkout - look for sale signs

8.99   SAVE
1.00
REG. 9.99
GIRLS'
T-SHIRTS
• SIZES 4-16
• VALID 06/16 7-20

There's one more thing you have to do to be a smart shopper. You need to use some basic math skills. These are skills that you already have. You can multiply, and you can subtract. That's really all the math you need to know. With these skills, you can figure out which deals will save you the most money. Then, you'll be able to buy what you want—sooner rather than later.

What will you do with the money you save being a smart shopper? You could save it; spend it on family, friends, or yourself; or find a way to help others.

A calculator will help you to add the money you save.

You will be amazed at how easy it is to save money when you start shopping smart. A dollar here or there may not sound like much money, but what if you saved a few dollars every time you went shopping? Your savings would really add up.

This book will give you the skills you need to become a smart shopper. Read on, and soon you'll be saving money at the same time that you spend it!

You have the skills to uncover great deals!

Do the Math!

People wouldn't bother to look for sales if figuring out their savings was difficult. The math that you need to do to save money is not hard. Often, a store offering a sale has already done the math for you. Even if the store hasn't figured out the sale price, however, you can easily do it yourself.

Picture a store that is offering a **discount** on some sale items. The discount is the amount of money that is subtracted from the regular price of an item to give you the sale price.

A sale at half-off means items are discounted 50 percent.

Everything in this store is...
1/2 OFF
the lowest ticketed price

Figuring a Discount

How do you find out how much a discount will save you? Figure your savings in two steps.

1. Multiply the **percentage** of the discount times the regular price. A percentage expresses a part of a whole and can be shown as a decimal. Twenty percent (also written as 20%) is the same as .20. Fifty percent (50%) is the same as .50.

   For example, if an item costs $29.95 and the discount is 20 percent, multiply 29.95 by .20 to get $5.99. A calculator will help you do the math. That's the amount of money you'll save.

2. Subtract your savings from the regular price: $29.95 – $5.99 = $23.96. The result is your final price.

Estimating

You can also **estimate** your sale price. Round $29.95 to the nearest dollar: $30. Then, think about the fact that 10 percent of $30 is $3. Twenty percent is double 10 percent, so 20 percent of $30 is $6. Subtract $6 from $30 to get $24.

It Pays to Look for the Highest Discount

Suppose you want to buy a pair of sneakers that regularly costs $40. Your parents ask you what store you'd like to shop in.

You know that two stores sell the same sneakers, but each has them for a different price. One store has the sneakers for full price. That one is close to your house. You want to make the shopping trip quick because there is a basketball game you want to watch on TV later in the day.

However, a store that's a little farther away has the same sneakers for 25 percent off. Should you make the longer trip?

It pays to look for the best discount.

Of course you should make the longer trip! If you buy the sneakers for 25 percent off, you'll only pay $30 for them. Think how good that will make you feel.

What about the game you wanted to watch? Will you miss the beginning of the game if you take longer to shop for your sneakers? There is an easy way to solve that problem. Try to allow more time for the shopping trip. Get an earlier start.

Discount on $40 Sneakers	Figure It Out!	You Pay
10% ($\frac{1}{10}$, one-tenth, or .10)	.10 x $40 = $4	$40 – $4 = $36
20% ($\frac{2}{10}$, two-tenths, or .20)	.20 x $40 = $8	$40 – $8 = $32
25% ($\frac{1}{4}$, one-quarter, or .25)	.25 x $40 = $10	$40 – $10 = $30
50% ($\frac{1}{2}$, one-half, or .50)	.50 x $40 = $20	$40 – $20 = $20

These cards all mean the same thing: A 25 percent discount equals $\frac{1}{4}$ off the price of an item.

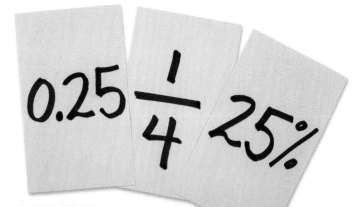

$0.25 \quad \frac{1}{4} \quad 25\%$

Discount Detectives Find Deals

Great **bargains** are everywhere, if you know where to look. Luckily, the search isn't difficult. Newspapers, catalogs, radio, and television all advertise sales. Holidays are a great time for stores to have sales. The start of a school year is another great sale time. School supplies are often on sale then. So are clothes and shoes for children.

Look for bargains around Presidents' Day in February.

You can also find great deals at grand openings and going-out-of-business sales. When a store has a grand opening, it wants to get as many customers as possible into the store. Low prices are one way to get shoppers into the store. With a going-out-of-business sale, everything must go. Even the shelves and lights may be for sale!

Different stores might have different prices for these in-line skates.

Take Your Time

All these sales are good news for shoppers because they mean lower prices. Once you have found a sale item, you don't always want to buy right away. To find the best deal, you need to compare prices between stores. Comparing prices is also known as **comparison** shopping.

You can find prices for nearly everything on the Internet.

Win the Comparison Game

Play a game with yourself when you shop. Try to find at least two different discount prices whenever you want to buy something. Once you have done some comparison shopping, you can head to the checkout with confidence. You will know you are getting the best price possible.

It's easy to compare prices with the help of the Internet. With an adult to help you, search the Internet for your chosen item. Once you have found the best price, ask a local store to meet this price. Many stores are happy to do this. Then, you will have the item right away instead of ordering it and having to wait.

Buyer Beware!

Sometimes a low price is too good to be true. Here are some things to watch for:

➡️ Does the item have all of its parts?

➡️ Is the item damaged in any way?

➡️ Is the item sturdy, or will it fall apart the first time you use it?

➡️ Be careful if a store says, "All sales are final." You won't be able to return it if there is something wrong. Is the item exactly what you want, and is it in perfect working order?

Before making a purchase, make sure no pieces have been lost and that the item works properly.

Remember, you will end up with extra money in your pocket if you are a good discount detective. You will amaze your friends when you tell them about the bargains you have tracked down. They'll beg to hear your smart shopping secrets. You'll soon be teaching them to become smart shoppers, too.

Amaze your friends with your shopping secrets!

Coupons Rule!

Did you know it's possible to save hundreds of dollars every year by using coupons? What's even better, you can turn some of those savings into dollars for you to spend.

Coupons are everywhere. You can find them in magazines and newspapers. Sunday newspapers are your best bet for grocery coupons and other items for your home.

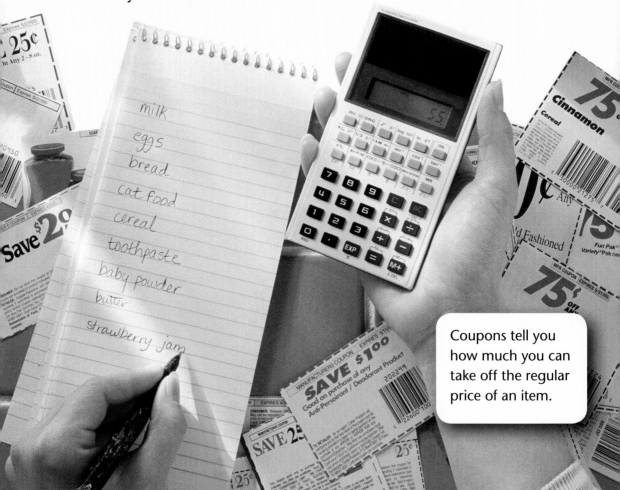

Coupons tell you how much you can take off the regular price of an item.

What will you do with the money you save on pizza?

The Internet is also a great place to look for coupons. Ask a parent to search for you. Nearly any kind of coupon you want can be found on the Internet. That includes coupons for toys, games, clothing, electronics, and groceries. People can even sign up for e-mail coupons.

Some coupons are worth more than others. A smart shopper compares deals to find the best one. Try it and see. Ask a parent to look for online pizza coupons to your favorite pizza place. Now, compare these to the coupons that come in your newspaper. Where can you get the best deal?

Grocery stores are bursting with coupons. Sometimes store workers hand out coupons with samples of food to get you to buy the product.

The coupon might be right on the item. For example, a $2.99 jar of spaghetti sauce might have a coupon that reads: "Save $1 now!" You can do a quick estimate to figure out that the sauce will only cost about $2 if you buy that brand. The cashier will subtract $1 from your total bill when you go through the checkout.

Look for coupons right on the items you buy.

Wouldn't spaghetti sauce taste better if you knew you'd saved money buying it?

You Can Help!

➡ Some special stores overseas for soldiers and their families, called **commissaries**, accept expired coupons. Ask an adult to help you locate some commissaries overseas. Then, hold a coupon drive in your class. Once you have collected the coupons, mail them to the commissary.

➡ Adults can search for Web sites that will donate to a **charity** when people use coupons from their Web sites.

➡ Use coupons to buy food for your local **food bank**. The food bank will distribute the groceries to families who need them.

Some stores may double, or even triple, the amount that is written on the coupon. This means double or triple savings for you. With a doubled $1 coupon, that $2.99 jar of spaghetti sauce now costs only $0.99!

With your parents' help, make a list of items that your family purchases regularly. Search for coupons and sales for these products. You can do this in just a few minutes each week.

Help save money on your family's grocery bill. Find coupons and information about sales in your local newspaper.

Turn Coupons Into Savings

Ask your parents if they would be willing to share the savings with you. Perhaps you and your parents could each get 1/3 of the savings. You could donate the remaining 1/3 to a food bank or other charity. With grocery savings of just $15 per week, your parents, you, and the local food bank would each earn $260 in just one year! (That's $15 times 52 weeks, divided by 3.)

Your savings are only limited by the number of coupons you find and use. Many people who use grocery coupons save hundreds of dollars every year.

Coupon Savings per Week	Savings in One Year
$5	$260
$10	$520
$20	$1,040

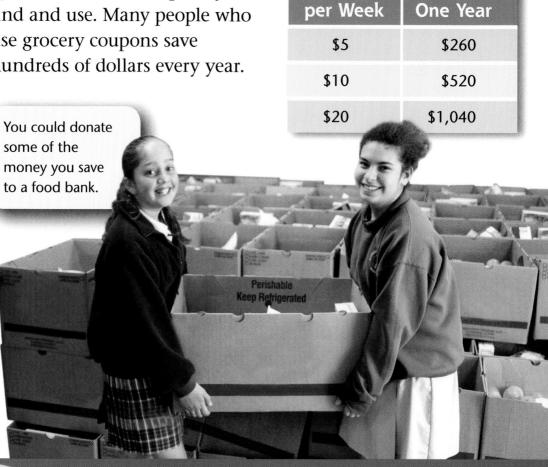

You could donate some of the money you save to a food bank.

Small Savings Add Up

What would be the easiest way to save for a skateboard that sells for $60? Most people would agree that the easiest way to save lots of money is bit by bit. It's usually harder to save in big chunks.

Look what happens when your favorite video store gives you a coupon good for a month. With this coupon, every video rental is 1/3 off. A video that normally rents for $3 will cost 1/3 less, or $2.

Your family might rent 2 videos a week, for a total of 8 videos a month. You will save $8 that month on video rentals. What will your family do with that $8? You could ask your parents to put it in a bank account for you. You could save it for the skateboard you want.

Get what you want sooner by being a smart shopper.

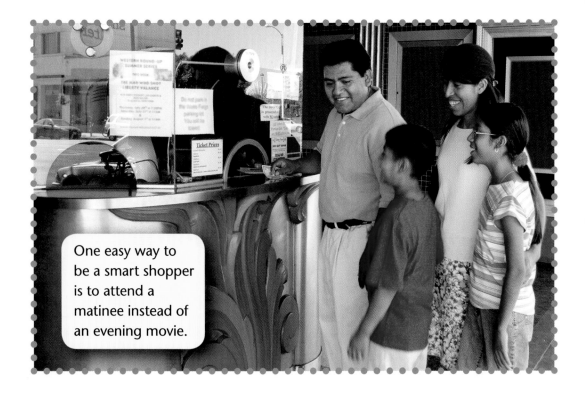

One easy way to be a smart shopper is to attend a matinee instead of an evening movie.

Time Can Be Money

Do you go to movies with your family? Do you ever go on Friday or Saturday nights? If you do, you should know that admission to a **matinee** costs less than admission to an evening movie. Ask your family if they would like to go to the movie on a Saturday or Sunday afternoon instead. You will all end the week with more money in your pockets. You could use the money you saved to go bowling or roller-skating. You may be able to do two things instead of just one.

Whatever your savings goal is, remember that little savings add up. Watch your savings grow!

Put Your Skills to Use

You are ready to put your new skills to use. You know where to look for bargains. You know that it is important to compare one deal to another. You know how small savings add up over time. You know how to check to make sure you are getting a good deal, too.

find sales **+** compare prices **=** big savings

The next time you shop, see how much money you can save. You will feel that you've really accomplished something important. Go ahead, be a smart shopper!

Don't forget to tell your friends about the bargains you've found and the money you have saved. You might be helping them to save, too. Sharing what you've learned makes sense. You could even say it "makes cents"!

How much would you pay for this pair of $25 jeans with discounts of 50%, 20%, and 10%?

Regular Price	Discount	Final Price
$25	50%	?
$25	20%	?
$25	10%	?

(answers on page 24)

Glossary

bargains   items offered for sale or a low price

charity   a fund or organization for helping people

commissaries   stores that sell groceries, household items, and other products to members of the military

comparison   weighing the value of one item against another

discount   the amount that is subtracted from the regular price of an item to give you the sale price

estimate   to find an answer that is close to the exact answer

food bank   a place where food is donated and then offered to people at no cost

markups   additional amounts of money that stores charge over what items have cost them

matinee   an afternoon performance or showing, such as a movie

percentage   a part of each hundred

Index

answers to questions on page 22: At 50% off you would pay $12.50 ($25 – $12.50); at 20% off you would pay $20 ($25 – $5); at 10% off you would pay $22.50 ($25 – $2.50).